The Effective Bible Teacher

By Josh Hunt

If you would like to be an Effective Bible Teacher, you might check out the lessons, Good Questions Have Groups Talking. Available at www.mybiblestudylessons.com

Table of Contents

Special Thanks

Special thanks to the following people for help with this book:

Kathy Weiser

Donna Stewart

Ace Sligar

Donna Stewart

Mark Lott

Denette Engle Hales

Pat Wilkes

Benji Thomas

Kellie Sharpe

Missy Hunt

The Need of the Hour

We desperately need an army of Effective Bible Teachers. What is an Effective Bible Teacher?

An Effective Bible Teacher teaches so that people live according to the Bible. Effective Bible Teachers create doers of the Word and not hearers only. Effective Bible Teachers make disciples.

Effective Bible Teachers result in classes that pray, people who serve, and individuals who read their Bibles and follow what it says.

Effective Bible Teachers create people who love the Lord God with all their heart, soul, mind, and strength. Effective Bible Teachers lead people to know their spiritual gifts and serve according to their gifting. Effective Bible Teachers teach people to abide in Christ.

Effective Bible Teachers love the people in their group. They hang out with them. They serve them. They have them in their homes. They are with them.

Effective Bible Teachers lead people to love. They lead people to lay down their lives in service to others. They lead people to care.

Effective Bible Teachers lead people to love the Word as they love the Word. The Psalmist said it is sweeter than honey. In another place, "Oh how I love your law." It was not mere duty and obligation. It was a delight.

Effective Bible Teachers make a difference. Their classes are different because of the way they teach. Their people are different because of their influence on the lives of individual members. Their corner of the world is different because it is infected by people who are salt and light.

People who listen to Effective Bible Teachers love it. They can feel their hearts changed each week as they are exposed to the effective teaching of the Word of God. They look forward to getting together. They rarely miss.

When they are in the group, they don't look at their watches. They don't fiddle with their keys. They don't day-dream. They are engaged, interested, thinking, participating, disagreeing.

They often find themselves with their hand up. Sometimes they blurt out things because they just feel they have to participate. They have experienced the truth of the Proverb that says:

> *The tongue of the wise makes knowledge attractive. Proverbs 15:2a (HCSB)*

The Living Bible is characteristically fresh:

> *A wise teacher makes learning a joy. Proverbs 15:2 (TLB)*

Things are quite different in the group that does not have an Effective Bible Teacher. Attendance is sporadic. People often arrive late. They look at their feet a lot. There is not much energy in the

room. People rarely speak up unless called upon. They never write anything down.

We need an army of Effective Bible Teachers. It does not matter if they teach in a home group or in an on-campus Sunday School class. What matters is that the teacher is an Effective Bible Teacher. It doesn't matter if they lead a children's class or an adult class. Obviously, specific methods would have to be different in each case. What matters is that the teaching is effective.

Why We Need Effective Bible Teachers

Bill Hybels has a saying that I just love: "We are going to teach our way out of this problem." Here is what he means.

Suppose you have a giving problem in your church. You are not meeting budget. You are not able to meet expenses. You have bills that are unpaid. You have cut back everywhere possible, but there are still bills to be paid.

More than that, there are missed opportunities. There are ministries to launch. There are needs that need to be met. The fields are white unto harvest if you could just get the money to buy the tractors. How do you solve this problem?

You could organize a campaign. You could hire a consultant. You could put up posters and send out letters. Those things may have their place. Bill Hybels would suggest you do something else: teach your way out of this problem. Whatever problems you have in your church, Effective Bible Teaching is a big part of the solution.

Perhaps the need is not so much money as volunteers. Every church I know could use an infusion of volunteers. Jesus said *the harvest is plentiful; the workers are few*. The bottleneck of the evangelistic / disciple-making process has always been and always will be workers.

Big churches need more workers. I had a man in a large church say to me once, "Do you have any idea how many workers you need to staff a Sunday School of 3500 people?"

Small churches need more workers. I pastor a very small church in the country. It is what we used to call a preaching point. Twenty or thirty people—mostly farmers—gather each week to worship and study the Word of God. Do you know what the need is at our small church?

Workers.

And how do we get more workers? Jesus said the answer is prayer. (Matthew 9.37—38) I don't take that to mean that we are to pray and do nothing

6

else. I take it to mean that nothing else will matter until we pray. In the next breath, Jesus said, "Go! I am sending you out. . ." I see two things in that passage: pray and send out.

There is a third thing that will help: teach. Teach on the joy of serving. Teach on spiritual gifts. Teach on laying down your life. Teach on finding life by losing yourself in the service to others.

One way to implement this is to organize a church wide campaign where you coordinate three things around the theme you are trying to emphasize:

- Sermons
- Bible teaching in small groups
- Daily quiet time

The classic example of this is the Purpose Driven Life Campaign. It is a model of what can be done by organizing sermons, Bible teaching in small groups and daily quiet times around one theme. (By the way—I have on occasion helped churches with the Bible lessons in a campaign like this. Contact me if you are interested.) josh@joshhunt.com

Does your church have a *giving* problem? Teach your way out of it.

Does your church have a *lack of workers* problem? Teach your way out of it.

Whatever problem your church faces, you would do well to follow the advice of Bill Hybels: teach your way out of it.

Let's zoom back the lens. Think about the capital-C Church as a whole. Here are four problems we need to teach our way out of.

Ignorance

Numerous studies have demonstrated the lack of Bible knowledge both in and out of the church. I had a man say to me once: "Joseph. . . he had that coat of many colors, right?"

"Right."

"And that was the father of Jesus?" We desperately need Effective Bible Teachers.

The Pew Research Center did a survey of basic knowledge of the Bible, Christianity, and world religions. Questions included naming the four gospels and whether or not the Golden Rule was one of the Ten Commandments. Curious thing about the results: atheists did better than church goers. To be fair, this was a survey of religious knowledge, not just Bible knowledge. Church goers did do better on the Bible questions. Everyone flunked.

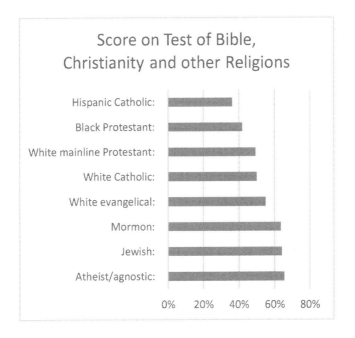

Church in decline

I have heard this stat for years: 75% of churches are plateaued or declining. Here is the latest: Based on our research of 557 churches from 2004 to

2010, nine out of ten churches in America are declining or growing at a pace that is slower than that of their communities. Simply stated, churches are losing ground in their own backyards.[1] Surely Effective Bible Teaching would help with that.

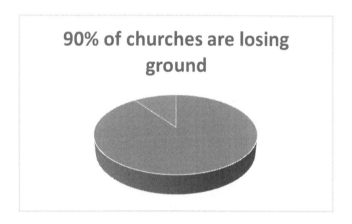

90% of churches are losing ground

With young people, the situation is even worse.

> *Another way of looking at it is generationally. About two-thirds of the Builder generation,*

---

[1] Rainer, T. (2013). *I Am a Church Member: Discovering the Attitude that Makes the difference.* Nashville: B&H.

those born before 1946, are
Christians. But only 15 percent
of the Millennials are Christians.
The Millennials are the largest
generation in America's history
with almost eighty million
members. They were born
between 1980 and 2000. And
we have all but lost that
generation.[2]

Surely Effective Bible Teaching would help.

Do church goers believe differently?

If we could get them to church, would it matter?
Let's look at this in two ways: first, we will look at
what church goers believe. Then, we will take a
look at how they behave.

---

[2] Rainer, T. (2013*). I Am a Church Member:*
Discovering the Attitude that Makes the difference.
Nashville: B&H.

Brad Waggoner reported the findings of a survey of church goers in his book, *The Shape of Faith to Come.* Here are some highlights of his findings:

- "The Bible is the written Word of God and is totally accurate in all that it teaches." About half strongly agreed.
- "Christians must continually work toward their salvation or risk losing it." Only 23% got it right.
- "If a person is sincerely seeking God, he/she can obtain eternal life through religions other than Christianity?" Only 32% got the right answer, disagreeing strongly.
- "Every person is born a sinner due to the sin of Adam being passed on to all persons." About half got this right and half got this wrong.[3]

Notice these are central doctrines of the faith and the survey is among church goers. Overall grade of

---

[3] Waggoner, B. J. (2008). *The Shape of Faith to Come.* Nashville: B&H.

church goers seems to be about 50%. That was flunking when I was in school.

Do church goers behave differently?

We are actually doing better than some people report.

It has been widely reported that there is no difference between the behavior of Christians and the behavior of non-Christians. That is not exactly right. Here is the more accurately stated truth: there is little difference in behavior between those who claim to be Christians and those who don't. Key words: "claim to be Christians." When we dig a little deeper and compare people who. . .

1) Claim to be Christians

2) Read their Bibles

3) Go to church each week

with people who don't do these things, some significant differences start to show up. For example:

- Christians live together outside of marriage about half as often as do non-Christians.

- Those who don't go to church were about 50% more likely to divorce compared with church goers.
- Christians are about half as likely to commit acts of domestic violence.
- People who attend church regularly are half as likely to commit adultery.
- Not only did Protestants commit less crime, but also the Protestants who attended church on a weekly basis did so far less than other Protestants. For example, 4% of the weekly attendees had been arrested, compared to 8% of the monthly attendees, 12% of the yearly attendees, and 15% of those who never attend.[4]

---

[4] Bradley R.E. Ph.D. Wright. *Christians Are Hate-Filled Hypocrites...and Other Lies You've Been Told: A Sociologist Shatters Myths From the Secular and Christian Media* (p. 145). Kindle Edition.

In every arena, active church attendance tends to predict good behavior, and absence of church attendance tends to predict bad behavior.

Still, the differences are not as great as any of us would like to see. Effective Teaching can make a difference. Imagine if everyone who attended church was engaged in thoughtful, convicting, Spirit-anointed teaching.

Between Class

There has never been a better time to be a Bible Teacher than today. This is true on several levels. For one thing, we have incredible tools at our fingertips that make Bible Study so much easier. Word studies that used to require Greek training, expensive books, and lots of time can be done with a few clicks on an IPhone—assuming you have the Logos app.

I want to focus in this short chapter on how technology helps us to prepare people for learning. (In another chapter, we will focus on how it helps us to shepherd the group.)

Why do people need to be prepared for learning? Howard Hendricks put it this way:

> *The Law of Readiness is this:*
> *The teaching-learning process*
> *will be most effective when*
> *both student and teacher are*
> *adequately prepared. It*
> *highlights one of the great*

problems for teachers: Their
students come to class cold.[5]

Do your students come in cold, or do they come in ready to learn—eager to discuss the topic of the day? Here is some good news: the Internet can help.

It could be as simple as an email asking them a question or making a request.

- This week we will be studying worry. Do a little Googling around to see what scientists have found about the destructive cost of worry.
- I am really excited about this week's lesson. (You are, aren't you?) We will be looking at the story of when Israel conquered Jericho. See what you can find

---

[5] Hendricks, Howard Dr (2011-11-09). *Teaching to Change Lives: Seven Proven Ways to Make Your Teaching Come Alive* (Kindle Locations 1689-1690). Random House, Inc.. Kindle Edition.

about what archeology has discovered on Jericho.

- Check out this video on the tomb of Lazarus. http//www.youtube.com/watch?v=K_n6RK hWqs4 Did you know it was still there?
- Ask a friend what he thinks it takes to go to heaven when you die.
- Who can bring snacks this week?
- Be in prayer for Bob and Tina this week. Bob's dad is in the hospital.

Just letting your group know you are excited about what you are learning and are eager to share can create a sense of excitement and anticipation. Obviously, you only want to do this sincerely.

It is a common thing for me to get really fired up when studying the Bible. You probably feel this way at times as well. Not a bad idea to fire off a quick email to your group letting them know of your excitement.

Sometimes the world tosses you a bone. Think back when Rob Bell released his controversial book, *Love Wins.* Nothing will stimulate learning like a little controversy. You might send out some excerpts and say you will be discussing this on Sunday.

The Shack was another book that grabbed our attention recently. It is also a good example of a book with some controversy. Stir up the controversy by saying you will be arguing about this on Sunday.

Sometimes, you will want to email individuals. Perhaps you have some readers in your group. If you are doing a study of Moses, you might ask them to read along in Chuck Swindoll's excellent book by the same title.

A lot of people receive four forms of communication on the same device: email, text, Twitter posts, and Facebook updates. You might take advantage of all four. A simple text that says: "Fired up about this week's lesson on forgiveness. You don't want to miss it!" could really boost learning readiness.

You might want to start a discussion on your group's Facebook group. You do have Facebook group, don't you? If not, they are free and easy to set up. Get your group talking on Facebook outside of class and see if it doesn't impact your discussion inside of class.

Sometimes you will want to call someone— perhaps your teacher in training. Every group should have a teacher in training who substitutes on a regular basis. Call him up and ask him to do a little research on part of the lesson you will be discussing. Have him teach part of the lesson based on his research.

Sometimes you want to have a face-to-face meeting. Here is a rule of thumb: every teacher should share a meal with every person in his/her class at least once a year. Tonight we will be going out to dinner with a couple from our Tuesday night group. Group time will always be richer because of it.

One more approach. Email your group and ask them to bring something to class. We did this at a fellowship for my home group. People brought little pieces of memorabilia that revealed something of themselves. It was a touching moment.

Class doesn't begin when class begins. Keep up with people during the week. Use email. Use Facebook. Use Twitter. Text. Connect. Keep up. Assign. This is life together. It has never been easier.

Before You Teach

Preparation is the key to almost anything. There is an old saying: success equals preparation plus opportunity. Teaching is no exception. Effective Bible Teachers prepare effectively. Ineffective Bible Teachers wait til the day before.

Read

Effective Bible Teaching starts with reading, rereading, and rereading again the Bible text.

Start early. Start the day after. If you want to be really good, read a few weeks ahead. I think you do well to read mostly in one translation. By doing this, your mind will near-memorize the text based on the rhythm of the words.

Occasionally read in other translations. Notice the differences.

Encourage your people to read. At the beginning of every series, my normal is to say, "If you are not reading anything else these days, join me in reading the book of James as we study this together." Most people need continual encouragement to read their Bibles. Nothing predicts spiritual growth like individuals getting into the Word for themselves.

You might, in fact, spend a little time in class talking about what people read. Ask: what did you learn about God? What did you learn about Christian living?

Most people say you ought to separate your daily quiet time from your time in preparation. The idea is you shouldn't always be reading the Bible for what it says to others. You should read the Bible for what it says to you.

I'd invite you to turn that idea on its head. Start with reading the Bible for what it says to you. Then share this with others. We only have so much time. I don't think it is necessarily a bad idea to read the text you are teaching on in your quiet time. For many Effective Bible Teachers, what they are teaching is an all-consuming life passion. Pray about that.

Read the text. Read it slowly. I sometimes read it backwards—start with the last verse, read a verse at a time from the end to the beginning. Read some context—a few chapters before and after. Read ahead into what you will be studying over the next few weeks. Effective Bible Teachers exude a familiarity with the text that can only come from living with it.

Study

Study is essentially bombarding the text with questions. I tend to go too quickly to the commentaries. Maybe you do too. If you want to be an Effective Bible Teacher you ought to say, "I noticed as I meditated on this text. . ." more often than you say, "The commentaries say. . ."

In the writing world, we like to speak of the six writer's friends. These are also the friends of Effective Bible Teachers:

- Who?
- What?
- Where?
- When?
- Why?
- How?

You might read through the text six times with these questions in mind. First read with the

24

"Who?" question in mind. Notice all the people in the passage. Ask, "What are they doing? What are they feeling? Why are they doing it? Where is this? When was this? How long ago?" Bombard the text with questions. Look for answers yourself before you depend on the commentaries.

This is not to say you shouldn't consult the commentaries. Dr. Curtis Vaughn taught me Greek. I remember him talking about a preacher he heard once who said, "I have consulted no man's books. I have looked at no man's commentaries. I have not depended on the words of man. I have only consulted the Word of God in prayer for today's sermon." Sounds spiritual, doesn't it?

He might as well have said, "I don't really care what God has revealed to others about this text. I only care about what God has revealed to me."

Here is an insight: you are not the smartest person, nor the most spiritual person to ever have studied the Word. To cut yourself off from the insights of spiritual giants down through the ages is just plain dumb. Your teaching and your people will suffer for it.

Again, we come to the word balance. Effective Bible Teachers prepare with a Bible in one hand and a commentary in the other.

Do your own study. Ask your own questions. Look for your own answers. Pray for your own insights. Then, read the best insights from others. What a wonderful word: both.

Apply

Study is about bombarding the text with questions and looking for answers—first your own answers, then the answers of others. The most important question is this:

Lord, what would you have me do about this passage?

Effective Bible Teachers are about making doers of the Word and not hearers only. They know it starts with them. Effective Bible Teachers often say, "As I studied this text, I was convicted that I need to. . ."

Paul said, "Follow me as I follow Christ." Effective Bible Teachers say the same. They set an example for their people to follow.

The example of obedience is current. It is this week. Your people want to know what Jesus is doing in your life this week. Effective Bible Teachers are being changed by the Word this week.

Effective Bible Teachers ask people to drink from a moving stream. God's work in their life is current. The constant prayer of the Effective Bible teacher is, "Lord, what would you have me do in responsive obedience to Your Word?"

It can be no other way. Imagine the opposite. Imagine a teacher who spends four or five or six hours studying, digging, preparing and yet, is not changed by the Word. What hope do they have of seeing others' lives changed?

What Is An Introduction To Do?

The very beginning point of teaching must grab the attention of people. It draws them into what they are about to experience in the Word. The introductory teaching persuades people to pay attention. It convinces them they need to become engaged in the discussion rather than check the weather on their cell phones. One way to do this is in the form of a promise:

- If you will give me attention today, I will show you how to forgive when forgiving is hard.
- Thirty minutes from now, you will be able to enjoy an absolute assurance of your salvation.
- I want to teach you today how you can worry substantially less than you do.
- I want to talk to you today about how you can break destructive habits in your life.

Notice a couple of things about these statements:

- They are application oriented. We are not out to make smarter sinners. We are out to change behavior.
- They have a "what's in it for me" orientation. This is based on a premise that is at the core of my theology: it is always in our best interest to live the Christian life. It is always good for us to follow God. God is a rewarder. We don't choose between God and the good life. Following God is the good life. (For more on this, see my book, *Obedience.*)

The worst kind of introduction

The worst kind of introduction is perhaps the most common: "Open your Bibles today to . . ." Most teachers who use that kind of introduction have an attendance problem.

This kind of introduction assumes people are interested. Happily, some of them are. I would be. If you used that introduction with me, I'd be fine with it. I'd gladly give you my attention to discover what the Word says in that particular passage.

But, the truth is, most people wouldn't be that interested. Most people are not staying up nights thinking, "I wonder what John 11 is about."

Consequently, people don't give you their full attention. They might look like they are paying attention. They are polite. But their mind is only half there. They are giving you what Linda Stone calls Continuous Partial Attention.[6]

Effective Bible Teachers want more than continuous partial attention. They want full-bodied, all-out attention. They want people on the edge of their seats. They want people to be fascinated by the gospel. Fascinated. Literally, their attention fastened. A good introduction is where that starts.

The Pre-introduction

Often, although not always, I use an introduction before the introduction. This is about rapport building. This is about connecting. This is about being human.

---

[6] http://lindastone.net/qa/continuous-partial-attention/

It is talking about the local high school football game. It is giving an update on the surgery. It might be talking about the weather or the latest news. It is about letting them know you are human and live in the same world as they do.

I am a big fan of video teaching. But, there are some things video can never do. Video cannot connect like a human can. Before you break open the Word, say hello.

Making the gospel attractive

Titus 2.10 says we are to make the gospel attractive. Attractive. The Greek word is *kosmeo*. It means to adorn. We get words like cosmetics and cosmopolitan from this word. Cosmopolitan Magazine is about being attractive. Let's tease out this meaning further.

I would like to introduce you to two kinds of word studies. These have only been readily available to the average person in recent years. They taught us to do these studies in Greek class. I remember thinking, "Well, that is really cool, but who has time for that?" Today, there is an app for that. You can do in seconds what it used to take hours to do.

31

In addition to looking a word up in a dictionary, I'd invite you to look at vertical and horizontal word studies.

- A horizontal word study looks at how this underlying Greek or Hebrew word is used in this translation in other places. (Stay with me; this is possible with no knowledge of Greek or Hebrew.)
- A vertical word study is when we look at how the various translations translate this word in this verse. Often, there is not a one-to-one relationship between a word in one translation and a word in another translation. Translators speak of a pool of meaning. By looking at a number of translations, we dip into the whole pool.

So, let's look at this word, *kosmeo,* as it is translated by the NIV in other places:

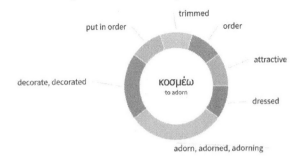

We see that this word has the sense of adorning or decorating the gospel. It is like tasteful makeup on a woman's face. It accents the beauty that is already there. This is what a good introduction does. Indeed, this is what good teaching does—it accents the full beauty of the gospel.

Let's look at a horizontal word study of *kosmeo.* Here is the rendering from a few translations:

- So that in every way they will make the teaching about God our Savior attractive. Titus 2:10b (NIV)
- Adding luster to the teaching of our Savior God. Titus 2:10b (MSG)

- In this way, they will make people want to believe in our Savior and God. Titus 2:10b (TLB)
- So that in everything they may adorn the doctrine of God our Savior. Titus 2:10b (ESV)
- So that in everything they may be an ornament and do credit to the teaching [which is] from and about God our Savior. Titus 2:10b (AMP)
- Then everyone will show great respect for what is taught about God our Savior. Titus 2:10b (CEV)
- Then they will show the beauty of the teachings about God our Savior in everything they do. Titus 2:10b (GW)

A good introduction—indeed all teaching—shows the beauty of the teachings about God our Savior.

Application-oriented introduction

The introduction may include a number of things:

- Stories
- Quotes
- Statistics

- Questions

But the key part of an introduction can be reduced to a promise. It answers the questions, "What will I get if I give you my attention today?" Or, stated differently, "What do you want me to do about what you are talking about?"

Doing is the key thing. James spoke of being doers of the Word and not hearers only. Teachers need to help with that, and it needs to start in the introduction. The Great Commission is about teaching them to obey. It is not about making smarter sinners.

What's in it for me?

Everyone is tuned in to radio station WIIFM: What's in it for me?

If you can show people how the teaching today will benefit their life, you will have their undivided attention.

But, isn't that appealing to selfishness?

The question reveals an underlying assumption. Allow me to reveal it in the form of several questions:

- Is it good for us to follow God?
- Is it always in our best interest to live the Christian life?
- Is God good?
- Is following God good for me?

If God is good. . .
If following God is good. . .
If obedience to God is always in my best interest. . .
If it is always good for me to follow God. . .

Then, there is no conflict. What is most glorifying to God is what is best for me. John Piper has a helpful quote from John Murray on this point:

> *There is no conflict between gratification of desire and the enhancement of man's pleasure, on the one hand, and fulfillment of God's command on the other.... The tension that often exists within us between a sense of duty and wholehearted spontaneity is a tension that arises from sin and a disobedient will. No such tension would have invaded the*

heart of unfallen man. And the
operations of saving grace
redirected to the end of
removing the tension so that
there may be, as there was with
man at the beginning, the
perfect complementation of
duty and pleasure, of
commandment and love.[7]

The introduction needs to spell this out. Reduce it to a sentence. Reduce it to a promise: if you really pay attention today, you will be one step closer to the abundant, John 10.10 life that Jesus promised.

---

[7] Desiring God: Meditations of a Christian Hedonist. John Piper

Reading the Word

My dad used to say: "You gotta know what the Bible says before you can understand what it means." We have to get the text itself in front of them.

People are shockingly ignorant about the Word of God. We have to get the text in front of them.

People are transformed by the renewing of the mind. It is the truth that sets them free. We have to get the text in front of them.

But we must be careful. I have talked to people who have sworn they will never go back because someone embarrassed them in a small group. Someone asked them to read the Bible when they weren't ready. We have to get the text in front of people, and we must do it carefully.

There is another reason we must do this with care. This is stereotypically the most boring part of the entire class. As much as we might hate to admit it, reading a chapter of the Bible together out loud is not always the most interesting part of a class.

We've got to get the text in front of people, but we must do it carefully.

Of course, there are easy solutions to these problems. Ask for volunteers to read rather than asking an individual to read. Once someone has volunteered, then you could ask them to read if you wanted. But taking volunteers is a safer route and should be the default mode.

Reading the Bible in small chunks is inherently more interesting than reading the Bible in long sections. Read in small chunks.

But there is a secret to reading the Bible in groups that every Effective Bible Teacher knows, and I want to talk about that now.

Give 'em something to look for

What made the Where's Waldo series of books so insanely popular? Why is the game "Hide and Seek" so perennially popular with children? What is it about looking for something that is just so much fun?

Well, I'll leave the philosophical answers to those questions to the philosophers. Let's talk about how we can put this basic human dynamic to work. We all love to look for things.

Here's the key: when you read the Word, give them something to look for.

Here are a couple of go-to examples:

- As we read this text, see what we can learn about God.
- As we read this text, see what we can learn about Christian living.
- This is a familiar passage. See if you can find something you've never seen before.
- It is always a good idea to read the Bible listening for emotions. I'd like half of you to listen for what David is feeling and the other listen for what Nathan is feeling as we read this passage.

  The key point is variety. This is true in how you read the Word, and it is true in just about every area of teaching. Predictability kills learning. The best way to read the Bible together is any way other than the way you did it last week. Here are a few

ideas to add some variety to your group
Bible reading:

- If you have someone with an especially
good reading voice, have him or her read
the whole chapter. You might email ahead
of time and ask him/her to be prepared to
read that chapter. The right person will be
able to read it with pizzazz and make the
text come alive.

- If it is a passage with a good deal of
dialogue, you might format it like a play
and ask several people to read various
parts.

- If it is a long passage, I have occasionally
asked people to read the passage silently.
Again, give them something to look for.

- There are great recordings of the Bible
available. I have one where the Bible is
read in dramatic fashion. Different actors
read different parts. The disciples are on
the lake, and there is a storm; you can hear
the storm in the background. You might
play an audio like this for your group. This
will actually do double duty. It will read the
text in a fresh way, but it will do something
else. Someone in your group will have the

idea, "Hey, I'd like to get something like that for my daily Bible reading."

- There is a cool app called Relax Melodies that has all kinds of neat sound effects - storm, waves, birds, rain on a roof, crickets, wind chimes, all kinds of stuff . . . iPad, iPhone, and Android versions, free and paid. If I ever have the chance, I will use it for background effect in Bible reading in a group. Such a great idea.[8]

- You might read short sections of the Bible together out loud. Of course, this only works if everyone has the same translation, but this is an easy enough problem to solve. Most translations are readily available online for you to copy, paste, and print for your group.

- It is not a bad idea to email your group from time to time and say something like, "We will be dealing with a great passage this weekend. But it is a little long. If you could read Psalm 139 ahead of time, it would be great."

---

[8] Kellie Sharpe

We have got to get the text in front of the group. Before we tell them what we think of the text, we need to get the text itself in front of the group. Don't assume everyone knows the passage. Often the power of the Word of God is in picky details in the text. We must read the text together. But, we must do it in a way that is interesting and does not embarrass anyone in the group.

Teaching the Bible

My day job is writing Bible Study Lessons. I have probably written more Bible Study Lessons than any human, living or dead. I write four lessons a week and have done so for years.

My Bible Study Lessons consist of about 20 questions with answers from well-known authors. If Max Lucado ever mentioned the Text we're talking about, I will likely find it. I'll provide a Max Lucado quote for you to use in class.

One of my favorite questions to ask goes like this: what did this word mean before it was a Bible word? Or, what did this word mean before Baptists got hold of it? For example:

- What did the word *saved* mean before it was a Bible word? We think of saved as having our sins forgiven and having a place secured for us in heaven. But often in Scripture the word saved is just an ordinary word. Jesus invited Peter to walk on the water. He did well until he looked around at the waves. Then, he started to sink.

"Lord, save me!" he cried. He wasn't talking about having his sins forgiven in this context. I don't even think he was thinking of heaven. He was thinking of not drowning. How does this story inform our understanding of what it means to be saved?

- The word *lost* is another great example. When we hear the word *lost* in church, we think of the theological category of lostness. We think of someone whose sins have not been forgiven. We think of someone who is separated from God. But in Luke 15, Jesus discusses three things that were lost—a lost coin, a lost sheep, and a lost son. One thing Jesus is teaching in these parables is what it feels like to lose something, and what it feels like when what was lost is found. Jesus seems to be making a big point of the emotion. In each case, he emphasizes the joy of finding what was lost. We also see the pain and desperation when something that is valuable to us is lost. One lesson is this: we ought to care about the lost, and think about the lost, and be a little bit obsessed about the lost, in the same way we get obsessed when we lose some money or our keys or a kid. My point is this: great insight can be gained by thinking of the word "lost" in its non-theological sense.

One more.

- *Redeemed*. We love to sing the song, "Since I Have Been Redeemed," and, "Redeemed, How I Love to Proclaim It," but do we ever use the word *redeemed* in everyday life? When I was a child, we used to redeem green stamps. But I am not sure that helps me to understand what redeemed meant in Bible days. Redeemed has come to be a strictly theological word. But, when it was used in the Bible, it was not a theological word. It was just a normal word. And so again, we need to ask, what did this word mean before it became a Bible word? The greatest picture of this is perhaps Hosea who bought back (redeemed) his wife who left him to live a life of adultery. Now there is a word picture of what it means to be redeemed.

We left God. We went after other loves.
We got ourselves in a mess. And God
bought us back at a great price.

What does it mean to teach?

What exactly does it mean to teach the Word of
God? This may seem like an easy question, but it is
one we ought to be very clear about. Perhaps the
best answer is given in the Bible itself. Let's look at
this rich passage from several translations:

- They read from the Book of the Law of
  God, making it clear and giving the
  meaning so that the people could
  understand what was being read.
  Nehemiah 8:8 (NIV)
- They translated the Book of The Revelation
  of God so the people could understand it
  and then explained the reading. Nehemiah
  8:8 (MSG)
- [They] explained the meaning of the
  passage that was being read. Nehemiah
  8:8 (TLB)
- They read from the Book, from the Law of
  God, clearly, and they gave the sense, so

that the people understood the reading. Nehemiah 8:8 (ESV)

- They read the Book of God's Teachings clearly and explained the meaning so that the people could understand what was read. Nehemiah 8:8 (GW)
- They read from the Book, from the law of God, translating to give the sense so that they understood the reading. Nehemiah 8:8 (NASB)

Teaching is about making the message of the Bible clear. There is a large gap in time between us and the Bible writers. There is even a larger gap in culture. Until we understand something of this gap, we will never really understand Scripture.

- We must understand what foot washing meant to them before we can understand what it means for us.
- We are told in Scripture that women are to cover their heads. Why is this? What did head covering mean to them? Until we understand what it meant to them, it is impossible to understand what meaning this has for us.

- There is a verse somewhere that speaks of tattooing. I have a preacher friend who was asked about this verse recently. The woman who asked did so because she didn't like tattoos and someone in her world—a child or grandchild—was getting a tattoo. She wanted a chapter and verse to say that this was wrong. In the same section of Scripture it also says it is wrong to pierce the body. The woman speaking had pierced ears. We tend to pick and choose. Effective Bible Teachers teach the whole counsel of God. They teach the meaning of God in its context. They help us to understand what the passage meant to them so that we can understand what it means for us. They make the passage clear. Clarity is the key point.

A lot of people are enamored by deep teachings. I have never really understood what is meant by deep teachings. I have never been accused in any teaching I've ever done of being deep. I am not bothered by that. To me, deep teaching is often just muddy. My goal, like the goal of the teachers in Nehemiah's day, is to make the passage clear.

We have essentially four tools to make the Bible clear:

- Explanation
- Illustration
- Object lesson
- Question-and-answer

We will talk about each one of these, but before we do, I want to mention something else.

Clear, But Not Too Clear

When I wrote my book, *Teach Like Jesus*, there is something I left out. Jesus' teaching was clear but not too clear. Jesus' teaching was intentionally vague at times. It was intentionally confusing at times. People are still arguing over what Jesus meant. It is my conviction that Jesus did this on purpose. He could have made it clearer. He could have made it plainer. He could have made it where no one would ever be confused. He didn't. Teach like Jesus.

Jesus disciples actually complained about this. In Matthew 13:10, we read, "The disciples came to him and asked, 'Why do you speak to the people in parables?'" Matthew 13:10 (NIV) The sense of it is, "We don't understand these parables." Jesus' answer is even more puzzling:

> *He replied, "The knowledge of*
> *the secrets of the kingdom of*
> *heaven has been given to you,*
> *but not to them.*

Whoever has will be given more, and he will have an abundance. Whoever does not have, even what he has will be taken from him.

This is why I speak to them in parables: "Though seeing, they do not see; though hearing, they do not hear or understand.

In them is fulfilled the prophecy of Isaiah: "'You will be ever hearing but never understanding; you will be ever seeing but never perceiving.

For this people's heart has become calloused; they hardly hear with their ears, and they have closed their eyes. Otherwise they might see with their eyes, hear with their ears, understand with their hearts and turn, and I would heal them.'—Matthew 13:11-15 (NIV)

Taken at face value, here is what Jesus is saying: if I didn't use parables, everyone might readily understand. If they understood, they might repent. Then, I would have to forgive them. I want to do that. So, I speak in parables.

There are some, I suppose, who are Calvinistic enough to think this is exactly what Jesus meant. But for many of the rest of us we are not sure. As one of my kids would say, "that just doesn't sound very 'Jesus-ical' to me." Indeed.

It is beyond the scope of this book to go into the depths of this passage. I simply want to point out that it is not all that clear. I believe Jesus was intentionally unclear. Teach like Jesus.

Effective Bible Teachers are clear, but not too clear. They intentionally leave some tension. They intentionally leave people arguing. Jesus did it all the time. In fact, they are still arguing.

There are not enough arguments in our Bible study groups. Do you disagree with me? Do you want to argue with me? Do you feel a certain energy in your soul that wants to speak up?

This is how we want people to feel when they listen to our teaching. We want them to want to raise their hand. Better, we want them to just blurt out because they can't keep silent.

I've heard people teach predestination as if there were no tension—no opposing points of view. From the teacher's viewpoint, it was all so simple. It's not simple, and people should feel the tension.

I had someone say to me once, after I preached a message from Romans nine, "If you push that idea too far, you will end up embracing predestination." Indeed. Predestination—the word is in the Book. R.C. Sproul calls it, "the doctrine everyone believes." What he means is that the word is in the Book. If you are a Christian, you must believe something about predestination. You have to believe in predestination. It is in the Book. You may not believe what R.C. Sproul believes, but you have to believe something. It's in the Book.

Want to know two magic words to enliven any Bible study group? Here they are: I disagree.

Walk into any sleepy Bible study group, listen to the discussion for a while, and then say these two words: "I disagree." Now, we are about to have a conversation. It won't be sleepy anymore.

I actually was a little stronger in a Bible study group recently. I turned to a man and said with a smile, "I think you're wrong. And here's why." He listened. Everyone listened. When I was finished, he nodded his head in agreement. No one looked at their watches.

I think he was changed that day. Just a bit. He was transformed by the renewing of his mind because someone confronted him. Someone said, "I disagree."

Jesus disagreed with people all the time. And they disagreed with him. And when they listened to Jesus, they disagreed with each other. They still disagree. Teach like Jesus.

Effective Bible Teachers have a little tension in their teaching. There is something about their teaching that makes you want to speak up. It makes you want to raise your hand. It makes you want to add your two cents' worth. It makes you want to correct them just a bit.

I'll bet you want to correct me right now. Am I right?

Story

Who is the greatest teacher who ever lived?

Jesus.

And how did Jesus primarily teach?

> *All Jesus did that day was tell stories—a long storytelling afternoon. Matthew 13:34 (MSG)*

A more straight forward translation:

> *Jesus spoke all these things to the crowd in parables; he did not say anything to them without using a parable. Matthew 13:34 (NIV)*

Notice that last line: He did not say anything to them without using a parable. Effective Bible Teachers never teach anything without some stories.

Why did Jesus use so many stories when He taught?

Perhaps He knew what brain scientists have just now discovered: our brain is wired for story.

Effective Bible Teachers include three or four great stories in every lesson. They include. . .

- Touching stories
- Shocking stories
- Funny stories
- Interesting stories
- Puzzling stories
- Lots and lots of stories

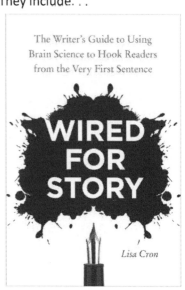

It would be good to have a story from the Old Testament in every lesson. You teach the Bible truth and you teach the Old Testament at the same time.

It would be good to have a story from your own life in every lesson. A story from your own life makes the truth real.

It would be good to have a story from the news in every lesson. Jesus taught this way. Remember when He said, "and those men who died when the tower of Siloam fell. . ." (Luke 13.2 – 5) Teach like Jesus.

It would be good to have a thoroughly hilarious story in every lesson. I heard someone say, "It is the rare communicator who can connect with an audience without humor." You don't have to be a standup comic, but a little humor goes a long way in connecting with an audience. One funny story could greatly improve any lesson.

One area where we probably have too many stories is from the farm. Unless you teach in a church like mine—which actually sits in the middle of the farm—you probably don't teach to all that many farmers. Jesus told a lot of stories from the farm because it was an agrarian society. There were lots of farmers. We have too many stories from the farm and not enough stories from the news.

It is always interesting to imagine how Jesus would tell a story if He were telling it today. In the story of the prodigal son we read, "He went off to the far country." We don't talk like that today. I think Jesus might say, "The boy ran off to Las Vegas." A little later it says, "There was a great famine." Ever been in a famine? An honest-to-goodness famine? Ever been to Wal-Mart and there was no food on the shelves? How would Jesus tell the story if he were telling it today? I think he would say, "There was a recession. Unemployment was high. Jobs were nowhere to be found."

Jesus told made up stories that sounded current. We should do the same.

What makes a great story great?

Effective Bible Teachers evaluate every story by two things.

- Is it interesting?
- Does it fit?

Effective Bible Teachers find stories that are compelling. They are mesmerizing. They hold interest. The mind does not wander. People don't look at their watches. People retell the story later, at work tomorrow. I can remember stories that I heard 40 years ago and you probably can too. The brain is wired for story.

But being interesting is not enough. In fact being interesting can be distracting if it is not something else: it needs to be on target. It needs to make the point. It needs to not distract.

I have been tempted at times to use stories because they were just so incredibly interesting. I just love the story and sometimes, I pushed the story into the lesson. Effective Bible Teachers never do this. They want compelling stories, but they want compelling stories that fit the message.

We are not just storytellers. There are conventions for that—where effective storytellers get together and swap stories. That is not what Bible Teaching is about. It is about making a point. It is about communicating truth. It is about changing lives.

Where to find great stories

At the risk of sounding flagrantly self-promoting, a quick and easy way is to subscribe to my lessons, *Good Questions Have Groups Talking*. They are available on a subscription basis or on Amazon in both print and Kindle versions.

Here are some other ways:

- www.sermoncentral.com I love the site. You can look up stories by text, topic, or type of story: funny stories, etc. I would encourage you to become a contributor and add your own stories.
- Made up stories. Jesus made up stories and so should you.
- Your own life. Every week in every lesson ask yourself, "What is a story from my own life that illustrates this point?" Balance is in order here. Not too many, not too few stories about your own life.
- Stories from the news. This is one of the reasons—one of the many reasons—you should start your preparation early. If you know early in the week what you will be teaching on you will find stories in the news almost every week.
- Movies. Same thing about starting preparation early.

- Story-rich books. Effective Bible Teachers are lovers of books. They love to hang out at Barnes & Noble. Most of them have a Kindle. And all this reading provides a rich resource to find great stories to illustrate God's truth.

Jesus never taught anything without using a story. Teach like Jesus.

Stuff That You Can Touch and Feel

I was privileged to hear Mike Dean preach recently. The big idea of the message was on service. We need to do more than sit and soak up Bible study lessons; we need to be doers of the Word. The Son of Man came not to be served but to serve. We too need to serve.

One of the great things about this message was the application. Mike gave lots of examples of different ways we can be involved in service. No matter your interest, your talent, your schedule, there is a way for you to serve.

The entire time Mike was speaking, there was a clear bowl of water in front of him with a large yellow sponge in it. With the bowl of water just sitting there, you couldn't help but wonder why it was there. Toward the end of the message he used it as an incredible object lesson.

Mike said that God doesn't want us just to sit and soak. When we sit and soak, we sour. Mike put his hand on the sponge. He dipped into the water. He squeezed it and let it go. He lifted it up and squeezed again. Water poured out.

Mike talked about how we don't want to sit and soak. He talked about how we all will be used by God. He kept dipping the sponge in the water and pulling out and squeezing it. I'll never forget that picture.

Object lessons are like that: we never forget them. I remember an object lesson from when I was in the sixth grade. I don't remember the preacher, but I remember the object lesson. The preacher pulled out a big barrel. He talked about Elijah and the widow at Zarephath—how "The jar of flour will not be used up and the jug of oil will not run dry until the day the LORD gives rain on the land." 1 Kings 17:14 (NIV)

I listened to that preacher for a whole year. I don't remember any other sermons he preached. But I remember that one because he used an object lesson. Object lessons stick to the brain.

Where to find great object lessons

What if you're not very creative? What if you can't come up with object lessons? I've got good news. Here are four sources of great object lessons:

- Google it. There are tons of sites with ideas for object lessons. Don't be afraid to look at children sites. If you keep the kids' interest, you will likely keep the adults' interest as well. (The opposite is not true.)

- Books. Similarly, there are tons of books available on object lessons. Many of them are geared for kids, but work equally well for adults.

- Your group's creative juices. You may not be all that creative, but there's a good chance someone in your group is. Email them and ask them for ideas. My guess is group will suddenly become a whole lot more interesting for them and everyone else.

- Form a group of teacher friends. The technology could be as simple as an email group where everyone simply hits "reply to all." Alternatively, you might make or join a Facebook group. If everyone is studying the same curriculum, all the better. In any case, you all have a similar interest: to make your Bible teaching effective. Swap ideas. Brainstorm.

Effective Bible Teachers use stuff that you can touch and feel. They use stuff that you can smell, taste, hold, manipulate. Such teaching is unforgettable.

Question-and-Answer

This is my favorite. I love a good Bible discussion. I love it when people disagree. I love it when there are different points of view.

It happened just the other night in our Tuesday night small group. The passage was one that relates to the topic of this book. It was the passage in James speaking to the idea that teachers will be judged more strictly. I have always thought of that as meaning judged by God more strictly. I have always taken that to mean that to some degree teachers are held responsible for the behavior of the people they teach. This is why it says, "Not many of you should try this." (That is my paraphrase.)

But someone in the group had a completely different take on the same verse. He posed the question, "Is this judged by God or judged by others?" I had always assumed it was judged by God. He assumed the opposite. He talked about how all of us tend to judge teachers more strictly. The text seems to support that. It seems to support my view as well. This is what makes for a great discussion.

The heart of the discussion is what I call the jump ball question. This is a question that can legitimately go either way. The truth is often a careful midpoint between two extremes. We must lead people to find the narrow way. Jump ball questions help us to do that. Here are some examples:

- Is Christian living easy or hard? Jesus said, "My yoke is easy, and my burden is light." Christian living is either easy or impossible. It is easy because it is not us living it. Paul said, "I have been crucified with Christ. It is no longer I who live but Christ who lives in me." Yet, the Bible says in another place, "we must go through many hardships to enter the kingdom of God."
- Is Christian living about striving and straining and trying really hard to be good, or is it about letting go and letting God? Is Christian living active or passive? Is it getting out of the way and letting God live His life through us, or is it trying really hard

to live a life He has called us to live? My answer? Yes.

- Does God save people against their will? Does God keep people saved who don't want to be saved? Can Christians misbehave as badly as they want and still go to heaven when they die? If God has predestined who will be saved, then does it matter whether or not we witness? Why do missions if God has determined who will be saved?
- Are we saved by faith alone? Are we saved by faith that is alone? If a person says he has faith in Christ yet never shows any fruit is he really saved?

The jump ball question is the heart of the lesson, but it is not the whole lesson. I write lessons for a living. I think I've written more lessons that any human, living or dead. Here are some question types I often use:

- What does the text say?
- What does the text mean?
- Who can locate Ephesus on a map?

- How does your translation have Romans 12.1?
- What are 10 ways we could serve our community? (Note: I am not asking for commitment at this point; just brainstorming.)
- How do you think the son felt as he approached the father near the end of the story? It is always a good idea to read the Bible with an emotional question.
- Can you think of any other verses that speak to the same idea?
- What does this passage teach about God?
- What does this passage teach about us?
- Why don't we do this more often?
- How do I become a person of faith and confidence?
- Yes, but how?
- How will it benefit me to serve? To give? To forgive? To be obedient?
- What will it cost me if I don't serve? What if I don't give? What if I don't forgive? What if I am not obedient? What will it cost me if I don't?

- What do you want to recall from today's discussion?

Just the right amount of silence

The key to making questions work is just the right amount of silence. Too much and it feels awkward and weird. Too little and people don't have enough time to think. It is in that quiet moment, when people are thinking that life change is actually taking place. Effective Bible Teachers have a feel for what is just the right amount of silence. Rule of thumb: it is likely a little more than you think. Most teachers, it seems to me, are afraid of silence. Sometimes I will say to a group, "Don't be afraid of the silence. Just think for a moment."

Handling wrong answers

If you use question-and-answer regularly, you'll regularly run into situations where people offer the wrong answer. There are several ways of dealing with this:

- If the answer is wrong but not particularly damaging theologically, sometimes I just let it go. I might say something like, "Anyone else?"

72

- If I know the group well, and especially, if I know the person well who gave the wrong answer, I might simply say, "That's not quite right." Caution: if you do this too often people will just quit answering. Here's another thing: if people are giving wrong answers all the time this is not a reflection of the class so much as it is a reflection on the teacher. School teachers who flunked the whole class don't have stupid kids, they are bad teachers. They either have not taught well or are simply asking questions that are too difficult. Asking questions is an art. People like to answer questions that are on the edge of their knowledge. If you ask a question like, "Who died on the cross for our sins?" No one will answer. It is too easy. If you ask a question like, "who was Melchizedek and why is he important to our theology?" I doubt anyone will answer that one either. (I am not sure I have the answer to that question.) People like to answer questions that they are confident are right but they also think that they are the only one in the room who knows the right answer. So a real key in asking questions is to ask questions that are hard enough to be challenging but that people actually know the answer to.

Wrong answers tell us something extremely important. They tell us what the group does not know. They inform us about the general level of knowledge that is in our group and tell us where we should be pitching our teaching.

We have over 100 recorded examples of Jesus asking questions. (I actually list these in my book, *Teach Like Jesus*.)

Effective Bible Teachers use question and answer constantly when they teach.

Application

Effective Bible Teachers teach for application. Relentlessly. Constantly. Aggressively. For Effective Bible Teachers, teaching is all about application.

In the Great Commission, Jesus said, "teaching them to obey. . ." Not, "teaching them everything I have commanded." But, "teaching them to obey." For Jesus it was all about application. Jesus' brother, James taught that we are to be doers of the Word and not hearers only. Amen and amen. How do we do that?

Brainstorm ways to be obedient

I make a distinction between application questions and commitment questions. Application questions are about brainstorming the various ways we *could* apply a truth to our life. For example, suppose we are looking at the verse that says, "Be kind one to another." Let's suppose we are making application around being kind to your wife. I might ask, "What are 10 ways a husband could be kind to his wife?" So, the list might look like this:

1. Buy her flowers.

2. Let her pick out the movie.
3. Wash the dishes.
4. Listen to her without interrupting.
5. Walk the mall with her.
6. Watch the kids.
7. Take her out on a date night.
8. Buy her chocolate. What woman doesn't like chocolate?
9. Buy her a card for no reason at all.
10. Vacuum.

Notice I have not asked the group to do anything (yet). I've only ask them to make a list of things they *could* do. Then, we asked them to pick from a list. We asked them to do one thing on the list.

Two magic questions

With this application in mind, Effective Bible Teachers follow up with two magical questions:

- How will it benefit me if I do?
- What will it cost me if I don't?

These two questions are based on a fundamental assumption I have of Christian living: it is always in our best interest to live the Christian life. It is always good for me to follow God. Obedience is always good for me in the long run.

How does it benefit a husband to buy his wife flowers or do the dishes or take out the trash or take her on a date night? Much in every way!

What will it cost you if you don't love your wife in practical ways like listening to her and serving her and buying her cards for no reason at all? Trust me, if you lose your marriage, you will spend the rest of your life regretting it.

God is a rewarder

Hebrews 11.6 is my favorite verse:

> *And without faith it is impossible to please God, because anyone who comes to him must believe that he exists and that he rewards those who earnestly seek him.—Hebrews 11:6 (NIV)*

God is a rewarder. It is impossible for me to draw near to God except that I believe that God is a rewarder. If God is a rewarder, I will be rewarded for seeking Him. It is always in my best interest to live the Christian life. It is always good for me to follow God.

This is important because we are all irrevocably hardwired to do what we believe to be in our best interest. The key word is *believe*. This is why faith is so important to Christian living. What we believe determines what we do. If we believe that God is good; if we believe that He is smart; if we believe that He has our best interest at heart; then trusting Him is relatively easy.

But if in my heart of hearts I believe that God is not good, that He can't be trusted, that He is not after my well-being, it is impossible—impossible for me to draw near to Him. Not because this belief that God is a rewarder is some kind of magic key that opens the door; it is simply the nature of things. I am irrevocably hardwired to do what I believe to be is in my best interest. I will only seek God if I really believe He is a rewarder.

I must come to love the Christian life or I will never come to live the Christian life.

The people you teach must come to love the Christian life or they will never come to live the Christian life.

Prayer must become for them a sweet hour of prayer, or I will bet they didn't pray this morning.

Service is either a joy or a struggle.

Self-control will only get us so far. We will only make it so far forcing ourselves to do what we fundamentally don't believe is in our best interest. Sooner or later we will do what we believe is best for us. We either come to believe that God is good, that God is a rewarder, that it is good for us to follow God, or we will not follow God very far.

There is a place in Christian living for self-control. There are times when we must force ourselves to do what we don't feel like doing in the moment. There are times we must force ourselves to give even when it hurts. But, we either become joyful givers or we end up becoming stingy, selfish, people.

We must come to love the Christian life, or we will never come to live the Christian life. This is the key to application.

Ask For the Big Order

There is a difference between teaching for application and teaching for commitment. We need both.

Teaching for application explores all the ways the Bible applies to our life. But it doesn't actually ask people to do anything. Teaching for commitment asks for the order. It asks for people to lay down their lives. It asks people to commit.

My observation about teachers is that they can be too timid. They don't ask for the big order. They don't ask for all-out commitment. In the words of Bill Hybels, "They don't make the big ask."

When you think of the church in America, do you think of an army of totally sold out soldiers of the cross? When you see the church as it actually is, do you see a band of brothers who are laying down their lives for the advancement of the kingdom? If you don't—as I don't—we have to lay part of the blame on the lack of Effective Bible Teachers who have failed to make a compelling case for the glory of laying down your life for the cross.

If you'd like to see an example of the kind of teaching I'm talking about, Google John Piper's message, _Don't Waste Your Life_. I have listened to it a dozen times or more. We need more teaching like that.

It Starts with Example

It starts with example. It starts with praying this prayer before your group almost every week:

> Lord, I come before You again and humbly acknowledge that You are God and I am not. You are Boss and I am not. You are Master, I am slave. Whatever You ask me to do, wherever You ask me to go, whoever You ask me to love, I will do, I will go, I will love.
>
> I do so joyfully acknowledging that you are God. You are smart. You know the end from the beginning. You love me. It is always in my best interest to follow You.

I repent of the belief of thinking
that I know best. I repent of the
belief of thinking that my ways
are best. Your ways are best.
You are smart and You are
loving. The only reasonable
thing for me to do is to submit
to Your good will.

Robust teaching

This prayer of commitment must be preceded (or followed) by robust teaching on the goodness, wisdom, and loving nature of God. We must teach with passion that God is good, that God loves us— that He loves us more than we love ourselves. And He knows far better than we know. He sees what will happen next week, next month, next year.

He is altogether loving. He absolutely has our best interest at heart. He loves us so much He was willing to give up the life of His Son so that we could have life. Our life will always get better—in the long run—as we follow Him. It is always in our best interest to live the Christian life. It is important—and I say it again—that we must come to love the Christian life or we will never come to live the Christian life.

Ask

Bill Hybels has a great chapter on why it is important that we ask for commitment. It is not enough to tell them that God is good and that following God is good for them. We must ask them to follow God with all their heart, soul, mind and strength. It is not enough to explore ways we could obey Scripture. We must ask them to do something. Here is why:

> In my own life, I've rarely made
> a sizable step forward—
> spiritually, physically,
> emotionally, or otherwise—
> unless someone asked me to do
> so. Along the way, I've radically
> altered my eating and exercise
> habits because exceptional
> leaders have asked me to
> consider becoming a healthier
> person. I've channeled
> resources toward worthy causes
> because courageous leaders

*have asked me to help them
achieve a compelling vision. I've
parented more intentionally,
supported my wife with greater
devotion, practiced spiritual
disciplines more faithfully, and
upped the ante on my own
leadership development, to
name just a few, all because
gutsy leaders asked me to do
so.[9]*

It is likely true of the people you teach as well. They won't become the prayer warriors that they need to become unless you ask them to pray. They won't spend time in the Word except that you ask them to set an alarm. They won't serve until you ask them to serve. They won't become better husbands, better wives, better dads, until you make the big ask. Boldly, clearly, joyfully, enthusiastically, make the big ask.

---

[9] Hybels, B. (2008). *Axiom: powerful leadership proverbs.* Grand Rapids, MI: Zondervan.

So let me ask you: do you regularly make the big ask or do you simply tell people about the Bible? Do you ask people to lay down their lives or do you simply convey biblical truths? Do you ask people to commit or are you satisfied to discuss biblical principles of commitment?

Will you? Will you ask them to lay down their lives? Will you ask them to pray? Will you ask them to serve? Everything will be better if you do.

Their lives will be better. Their families' lives will be better. Your church will be better. Your group will be better. And here is what is most important: God will be glorified.

Make the big ask.

Teach From a Living Stream

Bruce Wilkinson has an excellent book every teacher ought to read: *The Seven Laws of the Learner.* In it he tells the story of a seminary professor of his. He would often ride his bicycle by the home of the seminary professor. Sometimes early in the morning, sometimes late at night, he would drive by this professor's home. Through the living room window Bruce could see the professor poring over the books.

The interesting thing was this: the professor taught New Testament survey. He had been teaching this class for decades. He knew the material in his sleep. But he kept studying. He kept reading. He kept preparing for every class just as if it were his first.

Bruce asked him why he did this. Why did he spend so much time going over material he clearly already knew? His answer was classic: I want to teach from a living stream.

Everyone knows the water from a living stream is better. Fast-moving water is better than stagnant water. It tastes better and it is better for you.

The same is true of teaching. The teaching that comes from a learning heart is better. Your people want to know what Jesus is teaching you *now*. Have you talked to Jesus lately? Are you struggling in prayer this week? Are you straining toward the prize this week? Are you learning this week?

I have heard too many Bible study lessons that go like this, "Back in '74 I had a situation and God showed me..." This is not to say that we should never share stories from a long time ago. Jesus said it this way

> *He said to them, "Therefore*
> *every teacher of the law who*
> *has been instructed about the*
> *kingdom of heaven is like the*
> *owner of a house who brings*
> *out of his storeroom new*
> *treasures as well as old."*
> *Matthew 13:52 (NIV)*

Notice that last line: new treasures as well as old. This is what Effective Bible Teachers do. They share new treasures as well as old. They tell of pivotal moments in their own life when God showed them life-altering truths. These moments will never be repeated and are appropriately recalled often. But Effective Bible Teachers do something more. They share from this week.

- This week's learning.
- This week's prayers.
- This week's struggle.
- This week's service.

People want to know: has Jesus taught you anything recently?

The With-Them Principle

The Navigators have a principle they call the *with-them* principle. It is based on Mark 3.14:

> *He appointed twelve--*
> *designating them apostles--that*
> *they might be with him and that*
> *he might send them out to*
> *preach. Mark 3:14 (NIV)*

Jesus' method of making disciples was largely about spending time with them. It was discipleship by hanging around. The Navigators published an article in Discipleship Journal that explained it this way:

> *Go places with them, listen to*
> *them, talk to them, think with*
> *them, pray with them. Follow-*
> *up is not done by something,*
> *but by someone—not a method*
> *or a system, but you.*

If we think about discipleship at all, we tend to want to make it much more complicated than this.

We develop notebooks, we print material, we develop courses, we have people sign things, and we have people commit things.

Jesus' method of making disciples was largely about hanging around. Jesus realized that Christian living is more caught than taught.

Robert Coleman has an excellent book on this, *Master Plan of Evangelism*. In it he says:

> Having called his men, Jesus made a practice of being with them. This was the essence of his training program—just letting his disciples follow him.
>
> When one stops to think of it, this was an incredibly simple way of doing it. Jesus had no formal school, no seminaries, no outlined course of study, no periodic membership classes in which he enrolled his followers. None of these highly organized procedures considered so necessary today entered into his

ministry. Amazing as it may seem, all Jesus did to teach these men his way was to draw them close to himself. He was his own school and curriculum.

The natural informality of this teaching method of Jesus stood in striking contrast to the formal, almost scholastic procedures of the scribes. These religious teachers insisted on their disciples adhering strictly to certain rituals and formulas of knowledge which distinguished them from others; whereas Jesus asked only that his disciples follow him. Knowledge was not communicated by the Master in terms of laws and dogmas, but in the living personality of One who walked among them. His disciples were distinguished, not by outward conformity to certain rituals, but by being

with him, and thereby
participating in his doctrine
(John 18:19).[10]

Effective Bible Teachers do this as well. They spend as much time as is reasonably possible with their students. They go to lunch on a regular basis. They fellowship together. They stick around after church. They go out to dinner. They have people in their home. They practice hospitality, as the Scripture commands. (For more on this, see my book *Christian Hospitality.*)

Ineffective Bible Teachers are quite the opposite. They are more or less like school teachers. They are content to present the material and go home. They give their lecture, click their PowerPoint slides, and call it a day.

To demonstrate the effectiveness of this approach I simply need to ask a question: who is the most Effective Bible Teacher you have ever had? My wife

---

[10] Coleman, R. E. (2006). *The Master Plan of Evangelism.* Grand Rapids, MI: Revell.

has asked this question dozens of times in seminars where she teaches teachers. The answers are always the same. The most Effective Bible Teacher is not the one who lectured the best, or was the most polished, or the most articulate. The most capital effective Bible Teacher is always the one that followed the *with-them* principle.

I think about a teacher in my own life—Barry Price. He taught me about half the years through junior high and senior high. He kept moving up with me. He was the best Sunday school teacher I ever had. Funny thing about that though, I don't remember any Bible study lessons he actually taught. What I do remember is he had me in his home. He took me snow skiing with his family.

I remember one time he got stopped for speeding on a snow skiing trip. After the policeman left and we were on our way his young daughter spoke up in protest, "That bad policeman. He should not stop Daddy."

"No dear, that policeman did not do a bad thing. That policeman did the right thing. Daddy did the wrong thing. Daddy was driving too fast."

I don't remember any lessons Barry Price taught about taking responsibility or admitting that you are a sinner, but I remember what he said to his daughter that night in the car. I will never forget.

What about you? Do you spend time *with-them*? I think it is a good idea for every teacher to share a meal with every student at least once a year. There is one exception. Because sexual temptation is such a problem, I recommend you follow what I call the Andy Stanley rule: I am never alone with a woman. I don't share a meal with a woman. I don't take a trip alone with a woman. I don't counsel a woman. I never talk about anything personal with a woman.

With this exception, I recommend you make it a habit to share a meal with each of your students on a regular basis. Have them in your home. Do things together. Spend time with them. Effective Bible Teachers always do.

Technology

There has never been a better time to teach the Bible or lead a Bible study group than there is today. We have incredible tools for Bible study, for outreach, for discipleship, for keeping up with folks.

Email. If you are a Bible study leader, email is your friend. I recommend you email your group every week and tell them how excited you are about studying the Word and how you look forward to teaching on Sunday. You might want to assign someone in your group to write up prayer requests and email them to the group. My 92-year-old mother does this in her Sunday school class. You can email assignments. Ask them to Google around a little about this or that. Ask them to look for a picture or watch a video before class.

Facebook. Every group should have a Facebook group. It is a great way for the group to keep up with one another. Life is often about minutia. It is about details. It is about sharing the simple pleasures of life. Facebook helps us to do that.

Facebook can also help us with outreach. Imagine this: every group member checks in every week on Facebook. They update their status with something like, "great to be in small group this week." Or, "so looking forward to being with my best friends in small group this week. Why not join us?"

Okay, let's do some math. Suppose you have 20 people in your group. Suppose all of them do this. Suppose they check-in at the beginning of class and one other time during the week they post on Facebook something about their group. Suppose each of them has 1000 friends. (I have about 3000.)

20	People in your group.
X2	Updates per week.
X1000	Friends per group member.
40,000	People per week hear about your group per week.
X52	Weeks per year.

2,080,000	Times per year your group is mentioned to your group members' friends.

Bible Study. We have better tools for studying the Bible than we have ever had. I use the Logos program every day as I write Bible study lessons. Let's say this week's lesson is on John 11, the raising of Lazarus. If Max Lucado or John MacArthur or Charles Swindoll or Beth Moore ever said anything about the raising of Lazarus, I will likely find it and provide it to the teachers I serve. What a time to be alive! Logos makes it easy to do horizontal word studies—where I can find how this word is translated in this translation every other time it is used. They taught us to do this in Greek class, but it took so long I never actually did it.

I actually use WordSearch to do horizontal word studies. This is where I will look at 15 different translations and see how the translators translated a particular word in this particular verse. What a time to be alive!

Texting. As of this writing I may be the last person on the planet that has a cell phone that is not a smartphone. But my kids all have smartphones. On the same device they can receive a call, a text, or a Facebook update. I asked them recently which one they were most likely to respond to the quickest. Hands down, text.

Allan Taylor tells me they do a "can you hear me now" Sunday from time to time. This is where they contact prospects and absentees during class. They take a few minutes at the beginning of class to contact people. He emphasizes that you need to keep it really friendly. A friendly text from people in your group on a regular basis that says, "we missed you this week ;-)" might go a long way toward getting people to come back. It is free and easy and only takes a moment. What a time to be alive!

I recommend you set up a text group for your class and from time to time send everyone a text. Tell them you are looking forward to the lesson on Sunday. Tell them you are looking forward to the fellowship. Tell them the surgery was a success.

Keep up. Connect. It has never been easier. What a time to be alive!

Twitter. You can communicate with class members and prospects quickly and concisely using Twitter. These "real-time" messages, called Tweets, are limited to 140 typed characters. Once you get the Twitter account established, class members choose to "follow" you, and then they receive any Tweet you send. An added advantage is that your Twitter account can also be set to also automatically post to your Facebook page. That way, any Tweet you send will also be seen by your Facebook friends.[11]

How to learn any technology

I close this chapter with a section on how to learn any technology. Does it sound like I have overpromised? Keep reading.

If you want to learn any technology you just have to be willing to feel stupid. I often talk to people about technology, and they always say the same

---

[11] Mark Lott.

thing: "I don't know how to do that." To which I respond, "no one was born knowing."

I'm writing this book using Dragon naturally speaking dictation software. (Curiously, it did not get NaturallySpeaking right in the last sentence, although it did in this sentence. It is not a perfect technology.) I didn't know how to use this software until two days ago. Truth be told, I still have a lot to learn. But, I do the best I can, fumble along, make some progress, feel stupid, and before long I will be dictating three or four times faster than I could ever type. What a time to be alive!

You just have to be willing to feel stupid for a while.

My daughter got a new cell phone recently. I was eager to see it. I started clicking on a few buttons. Soon I felt frustrated. I could not figure out how to make a call. I could not figure out how to compose a text. I threw the phone down. No problem in this case, because it is not my phone. I don't need to learn to use it. You don't have to learn every technology. But you can learn almost any technology if you will keep the phone in your hands. Keep punching buttons. Keep feeling stupid.

Keep trying. Eventually, the lights will come on. You can learn almost any technology if you're willing to feel stupid for a time. If you don't have a Facebook group, click around, ask a friend, feel stupid for a while, and before long you'll be up and running. If you don't know how to text, remember this: no one was born knowing.

Technology can be a great friend to the Effective Bible Teacher. Of course, it can't do the most important things. It can't pray. It can't love. It can help you study the Bible better and quicker. It can help you keep up with people.

Did Anyone Learn
Anything Tonight?

I wonder if anyone learned anything tonight. I wonder if any lives were changed. It was enjoyable. I wasn't bored. I didn't look at my watch. But, I wonder if any lives were changed.

Effective Bible Teachers regularly ask these questions. They regularly evaluate. They constantly want to improve.

If I were in charge

If I were in charge of the Bible Study Groups at your church, here is what I would do. I would group the teachers into groups of three. As much as possible, I would try to put friends together. It would work better that way.

Let's suppose Tom, Bob, and George are in a group. A couple of times a year, I'd ask Tom and Bob to get subs and visit George's group. Then, I'd invite them to go to lunch together. I'd ask Tom and Bob to tell George a few things he did right, or the class did right and one thing that is not yet perfect.

Of course, Tom and Bob know they are coming next. So, they would likely be gracious with George. They wouldn't be too hard on him because they know it will be their turn next.

Feedback: the breakfast of champions

They say feedback is the breakfast of champions. Champions are always looking for feedback and ways they can improve.

Here is another old saying that is not quite right. See if you can figure out what is wrong with it:

Practice makes perfect.

Here is a more perfect saying:

Evaluated practice makes perfect.

We all practice things all the time and don't get any better at them. It is only when we evaluate and seek to improve that we get better.

Effective Bible Teachers are always evaluating and seeking to improve.

How important is this?

My research indicated about a third of our teachers drop below the bar of being even half-way decent. I am not talking about the bar of being incredible. I am talking about below the bar of half-way decent. Houston, we have a problem.

How many times would you go back to a restaurant where the food was not half-way decent one third of the time? How many times would you stay at a hotel chain where every third time the room was dirty?

Regular evaluation and improvement could move every teacher toward being an Effective Bible Teacher.

Ten questions to evaluate your effectiveness

Here are ten questions you can use to evaluate yourself as a Bible Study Teacher:

1. What was the level of energy in the room? Were people bored? Did they look sleepy? Did they look at their watches or fiddle with their keys?

2. Did I provide background information not in the text itself? Did they learn anything? Did they hear anything they have not heard before?

3. Did I teach for application? Was it clear what I wanted the people to do about what they heard?

4. Was there participation? Did everyone participate? Did anyone dominate?

5. Did I reduce the central truth to a pithy, memorable slogan?

6. Did I include a few good stories?

7. Did people laugh?

8. Was there a sense of the Holy Spirit's presence?

9. Was I as spiritually prepared as I needed to be? Was I prayed up?

10. What one thing do I want to do better based on evaluating this week's lesson?

Attendance

Effective Bible Teachers know you can only change people who are in the room. You can only make disciples of people who are present. Teaching is only effective when it is heard. God's Word only influences those who hear it. For these reasons, Effective Bible Teachers make considerable effort to build and maintain attendance.

Ineffective Bible Teachers just take whomever comes. They even spiritualize lack of attendance by saying things like, "Well, everyone God wanted to be there was there." Effective Bible Teachers don't see it that way. The way they see it is that the God who is not willing that any should perish is willing for all to be in the room to hear sound biblical teaching.

Building attendance involves two things: attracting new people, and keeping the people you have. In church growth parlance these are referred to as the front door (attracting new people), and the backdoor (keeping the people you have). In this chapter we will talk about attracting new people.

Invite, invite, invite

Attracting new people can be summarized in one word: invite. All things being equal, the more you and your people invite people to your group the better attendance will be. The research on this is pretty shocking. People are far more open to an invitation than most of us would imagine. It seems they are more open to responding to invitations than we are to making invitations.

This is an interesting point because of the teaching Jesus gave when He said, "It will be done for you according to your faith." Our faith—what we expect—is a positive predictor of what will actually happen. If we don't believe people will respond to our invitations, we are not likely to invite them. Let's look at the research on this.

Figure 2.1. The Rainer Scale

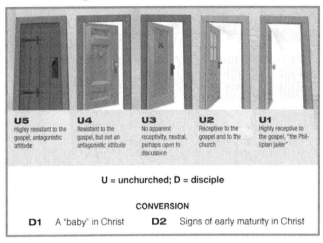

U5
Highly resistant to the gospel, antagonistic attitude

U4
Resistant to the gospel, but not an antagonistic attitude

U3
No apparent receptivity, neutral, perhaps open to discussion

U2
Receptive to the gospel and to the church

U1
Highly receptive to the gospel, "the Philipian jailer"

U = unchurched; D = disciple

CONVERSION

D1 A "baby" in Christ   **D2** Signs of early maturity in Christ

Thom Rainer divides the unchurched into five categories, ranging from U5 to U1. U1s are really open to an invitation to come to church. U5s are highly resistant. Let's look at the middle of the scale—what Rainer calls the U3s. These are the people who are neutral about Christianity. They are not hostile to Christianity, but they are not particularly receptive either. Here's what Rainer's research found about U3s' receptivity. "In the case of the U3s, 63 percent indicated they are "somewhat likely" to attend if invited. Another 23 percent said they are "very likely" to attend if invited. Do the math. Nearly nine out of ten U3s are at least somewhat likely to attend church if you invite them."[12]

Rainer says, "The research indicates that a simple invitation may be the most cutting-edge approach we can employ."[13]

Practical strategies to increase invitations

Here are some practical ways to increase the number of invitations to attend your group and your church.

- **Have an inviting campaign once or twice a year.** You can't emphasize everything all the time. You grow your group like you grow a muscle—tension and release, tension and release. Spend a month asking people to invite their friends and then back

---

[12] Rainer, T. (2009). *The Unchurched Next Door: Understanding Faith stages as Keys to sharing Your Faith.* Grand Rapids, MI: Zondervan.

[13] Rainer, T. (2009). *The Unchurched Next Door: Understanding Faith stages as Keys to sharing Your Faith.* Grand Rapids, MI: Zondervan

off. You might do a lesson once a year on the importance of inviting. The text is any one of several passages that has the phrase, "come and see." Thom Rainer's book *The Unchurched Door* is a great resource for this. You might make a game out of it and reward people who invite the most people. You might divide up teams and have a contest. Make it fun. Note that this is not an attendance campaign. It is an invitation campaign. We just want to encourage people to invite.

- **Invite using social media**. Ask every member to mention your church and your group twice on Facebook each week. In the group that meets in my home on Tuesday nights, three people in the group came directly from Facebook. Email, Twitter, and text can also be used.

- **Invitations using old-fashioned media.** In our attempt to be modern and hip and with-it we do well not to ignore old-fashioned ways of communication. The television didn't replace radio. The Internet didn't replace television. You would do well to send invitations through the mail as well as Email. You would do well to call people on an old-fashioned telephone and invite them.

- **Invite people to parties.** Have a party once a month. Do something that you genuinely consider fun. If it is not fun for you and your group, you will not be able to sustain it. The idea is not to dream up something that you imagine will be fun to outsiders. The idea is to take what you already think is fun and invite people to join you. If you like watching movies, have a movie night and invite outsiders. If you like watching football, invite some friends to watch football with you. Research is clear and overwhelming on this. The better outsiders know you and the people in your group, the more likely they are to attend your group. My own research reveals that groups that have nine or more parties a year are twice as likely to be growing when compared with groups that four or fewer parties per year. See my book, *Make Your Group Grow.*

- **Personal invitations.** Personal invitations are the hardest of all to resist. Invite members and prospects to lunch or to your home for dinner or dessert. One exception: I would never encourage men to invite women and vice versa. The stronger your relationship with outsiders the more likely they are to become insiders.

The Teacher As Shepherd

Jesus asked Peter three times, "Do you love Me?"

Three times he followed up with, "Feed My sheep," or, "Take care of My sheep."

There has been a great deal made over the subtlety of the underlying Greek word for love: *agape* or *phileo*. I don't think Jesus' point had to do with the difference between these two words. As writers and communicators sometimes we just want to use different words for variety, not for the subtle differences between them. I think the point was the repetition for emphasis. It was a way for Jesus to say to Peter: "Don't miss this."

I think Jesus was, in a way, talking to us. He was emphasizing the point so that you and I wouldn't miss it.

The passage says as much in verse 17 where it says that Peter was hurt because Jesus had asked the question three times, "Do you love Me." The point of the story has to do with the repetition.

And the repetition has to do with emphasizing this point: it is really important to Jesus that leaders take care of followers. We are to lead them. We are to feed them. We are to take care of them. We are to look after them. We are to keep up with them. We are to love them. We are to treat them like our own children.

An Old Testament Example

Ezekiel rebuked the leaders in his day with this scathing rebuke. Read it slowly. Read it twice.

> The word of the LORD came to me: "Son of man, prophesy against the shepherds of Israel; prophesy and say to them: 'This is what the Sovereign LORD says: Woe to the shepherds of Israel who only take care of themselves! Should not shepherds take care of the flock? You eat the curds, clothe yourselves with the wool and slaughter the choice animals, but you do not take care of the flock. You have not

strengthened the weak or healed the sick or bound up the injured. You have not brought back the strays or searched for the lost. You have ruled them harshly and brutally. So they were scattered because there was no shepherd, and when they were scattered they became food for all the wild animals. My sheep wandered over all the mountains and on every high hill. They were scattered over the whole earth, and no one searched or looked for them. —Ezekiel 34:1-6 (NIV)

What about the people in your church who are scattered—is anyone searching for them? An Effective Bible Teacher is very different from a school teacher in this regard. An Effective Bible Teacher is a shepherd to God's people, not merely a dispenser of information.

Let's get specific

Here are some specific activities that Effective Bible Teachers routinely practice:

- Develop a system for contacting absentees. I recommend you talk about this in class. Be honest about the fact that it is possible for any of us to slip into inactivity. Ask: how do you want to be treated when you are absent? We have a lady in our Tuesday night group who dropped out of church for a time because she was absent for a few weeks, no one contacted her, it hurt her feelings, and she dropped out. The system might be something along these lines. First week of absence do nothing. Two weeks in a row absent, message on Facebook, "Missed you last couple of weeks." After three or four weeks of being absent, call. Software can really help with this. The research indicates that if you do not contact people within the first six weeks of their becoming inactive you will likely never get them back. Time is of the essence. Develop a system and keep with it.

- Have a party once a month. Invite every member and every prospect. This will ensure that absentees get contacted once a month. It is sometimes difficult to do this without nagging, or coming across like a policeman or school principal. A friendly phone call once a month to say, "Hey, a bunch of us are going to go to a movie this Friday night. We'd love to see you!" Again, make it sure something you genuinely enjoy doing. Andy Stanley has a phrase I just love: "We would do this anyway." He is speaking of attending small groups when he says this. His point is that he would attend a small group even if he were not the pastor. He basically likes small groups. He would do it anyway. You need to feel the same way about your fellowships. Find some things you love doing, and invite every member to keep up with them, and every prospect to include them.
- Get in the habit of checking people's Facebook profiles regularly. Keep up with what is going on in their lives.
- Some teachers enjoy talking on the phone. If this is you, call your group members from

time to time just to chat. You might ask them about prayer requests. You might pray with them over the phone.

- If you teach kids, attend their events. If you watch them play basketball on Friday night there is a good chance they will be in Bible study on Sunday.

- Do something personal and individual with everyone in your group at least once a year. Have them in your home or take them out to eat.

- Send a group text to the entire group from time to time. One way to do this is to send a text (or email) as you are studying. Hopefully, from time to time you will get really fired up about the lesson. This is a great time to fire off an email or text and say, "I am really fired up about this week's lesson." Because this goes to everyone, it is not nagging absentees for not attending. It is just another way to make them feel included in the group.

- Visit members in the hospital.

- A proven and sustainable way to build fellowship in a larger class is what is sometimes called dinner six. The idea is to group six people (three couples) for one month. Sometime during this month the couples are to go out to dinner together or spend an evening in one of their homes. These smaller fellowship groups are really effective in strengthening bonds of relationship.

- Share the love. You don't have to do all of this yourself. Develop a team who will help you care for the people in your group.

Closing Thoughts

I'd like to leave you with a paraphrase of one of Bill Hybels's most famous quotes:

> *I believe that the local church is the hope of the world and its future lies primarily in the hands of its leaders.*

The church exists on three levels. It exists as an invisible, universal church. It exists as we classically think, a local church. And it exists as a small group. We see this in the New Testament where it says that the church met in temple courts and house to house (Acts 2:46). In big group meetings at the temple, and in small group meetings from house to house. Both meetings were the church. The large, temple court meeting with Peter preaching was the church. And the small group meeting in a home was the church. Your small group meeting in your home is the church. Your Bible study group meeting at your church's building is the church. And you are the pastor—the shepherd of that group.

One term I have used to communicate this is *micro church.* Your small group is a microcosm of the church. Most of what happens in a church — teaching, loving, sharing, encouraging, forgiving— happens in micro-churches—small groups. It is not an organization of the church, it is the church in its smallest form.

Now, to paraphrase Bill Hybels's saying:

> *The micro church is the hope of the world and its future lies in the hands of Effective Bible Teachers.*

May God richly bless as you serve His kingdom teaching a group effectively.

61348842R00074

Made in the USA
Lexington, KY
08 March 2017